THE WORLD'S GREATEST ELEPHANT

Ralph Helfer   *illustrated by* **Ted Lewin**

PHILOMEL BOOKS

To my sister, Cathi.

—*R.H.*

*To my editor, Patti Gauch,
who shared my passion for this project.*

—*T.L.*

The editors wish to acknowledge the creative assistance of
Emily Heath in the production of this book.

PHILOMEL BOOKS
A division of Penguin Young Readers Group.   Published by The Penguin Group.
Penguin Group (USA) Inc., 375 Hudson Street, New York, NY 10014, U.S.A.
Penguin Group (Canada), 90 Eglinton Avenue East, Suite 700, Toronto, Ontario,
     Canada M4P 2Y3 (a division of Pearson Penguin Canada Inc.)
Penguin Books Ltd, 80 Strand, London WC2R 0RL, England.
Penguin Ireland, 25 St. Stephen's Green, Dublin 2, Ireland (a division of
     Penguin Books Ltd.)
Penguin Group (Australia), 250 Camberwell Road, Camberwell, Victoria 3124,
     Australia (a division of Pearson Australia Group Pty Ltd).
Penguin Books India Pvt Ltd, 11 Community Centre, Panchsheel Park,
     New Delhi - 110 017, India.
Penguin Group (NZ), Cnr Airborne and Rosedale Roads, Albany,
     Auckland 1310, New Zealand (a division of Pearson New Zealand Ltd).
Penguin Books (South Africa) (Pty) Ltd, 24 Sturdee Avenue, Rosebank,
     Johannesburg 2196, South Africa.
Penguin Books Ltd, Registered Offices: 80 Strand, London WC2R 0RL, England.

Library of Congress Cataloging-in-Publication Data
Helfer, Ralph.
The world's greatest elephant / Ralph Helfer ; illustrated by Ted Lewin.   p. cm.
1. Modoc (Elephant)—Juvenile literature. 2. Circus animals—Juvenile literature.
3. Human-animal relationships—Juvenile literature. 4. Gunterstein, Bram—
Childhood and youth—Juvenile literature. I. Lewin, Ted. II. Title.
GV1831.E4H44 2006   791.3'2'0929—dc22   2005006490
ISBN 0-399-24190-6
10 9 8 7 6 5 4 3

ong ago, on a farm near the little town of Zezeldorf, Germany, a child and an elephant were born at precisely the same hour as the old church clock struck midnight.

"I will name my beautiful son Bram," said the elephant trainer, Josep, as he held the newborn child. "And as for this wonderful baby?"

A smile crossed Josep's face. "We'll name her Modoc. I can only hope these two will always be together."

And indeed, from that day on, Bram and Modoc were inseparable. They shared the same bottle as best they could and chased each other helter-skelter through the hay.

As they grew older, they accompanied Bram's father to the circus. The Wundercircus was a small German circus, famous for its performing pachyderms. People came from far and wide to see them, and Josep had trained them all.

"Someday you will take my place," Josep told little Bram, "and the whole world will applaud you and Modoc."

The years flew. When Bram and Modoc turned five years old, "Mosey," as Bram called her, weighed two thousand pounds, and when they were ten, she weighed four thousand while Bram barely tipped the scale at forty. Mosey was the biggest elephant in the circus, bigger even than her mother, and soon Josep put her and Bram into his act. The crowds went mad with excitement when Bram stood towering on top of Modoc's head.

At night, staring into Mosey's eyes, Bram sometimes thought that he and the elephant could read each other's thoughts. "We'll never be separated," he promised his friend. "No matter what happens."

But not long after that, the tents of the Wundercircus were abuzz. The circus had been sold! The new owner, a stout, pompous man named Jay North, spoke to the worried employees of the Wundercircus.

"The circus will be moving to New York," he told the crowd. "You will no longer be needed."

Bram went to the new owner the next day and begged Mr. North to keep him on as Modoc's trainer, but Mr. North refused to listen.

"That's a man's job. Can't have a kid like you trying to fill a man's shoes. Now git, or I'll call security!"

Bram was dismayed. His father was very ill now, and it was his last wish to see Mosey and Bram go to New York together. That night, he told his father a white lie. "Mr. North promised he would think about it," he said.

Josep died the next day and was buried in the old Grenchin Hill cemetery. All the circus people went to pay their respects. The calliope and its oom-pah-pah music echoed down into the valley. Bram rode Modoc down to join them at the gravesite. With her trunk, Modoc gently lifted a wreath from around her neck and placed it on the grave.

Bram had lost his father, and he was determined not to lose his best friend as well. With the help of a sailor friend, he hatched a daring plan. He would stow away on the boat that was taking Modoc to New York! Once they were in America, perhaps he could get a job as a roustabout—anything to be near Mosey.

So Bram hid, first in a truck, then in a packing crate full of circus equipment that was loaded onto the ship to New York.

It was pitch dark in the crate, and hard to breathe, but all Bram could think about was Mosey. Where was she? Was she afraid? The two of them had never been apart for this long in their lives.

At last, Bram's sailor friend, Jimmy, appeared. Jimmy helped Bram out of the crate, brought him some food, and guided him through the dark ship to the hold where the elephants were being kept. When Modoc spotted her friend, she gave a deafening trumpet.

Bram stayed in the hold with the elephants for the next few weeks, sharing the fruits and vegetables brought to them and hiding in the hay whenever the keepers came by.

Then one day, Bram noticed that it was difficult to stand up without holding on to something. Even the elephants were having a hard time keeping their feet.

Then a message came over the ship's loudspeaker:

"Attention! We are encountering high seas. No one is allowed on deck unless ordered."

At first Bram wasn't worried. How could a ship as big as this one sink? But as hours passed, the ship began to roll more and more violently. A trickle of water made its way down to the hold. Soon the trickle became a small river. The elephants were growing nervous.

Bram went to Mosey. "It's okay, girl," he murmured, then looked around. Mo and the other elephants were chained to the hold, but Bram had seen the keepers unlock them to clean the area. He knew where the keys were kept.

Hurriedly he found them and began to set his friends free. At last he went to unlock the chains that held Modoc. The water was so deep now that the locks were submerged. Bram fumbled with the keys . . . and dropped them in the swirling water!

With both hands he searched, but the waves had swept the keys away. Modoc strained against her chains, but they were so heavy and thick, even she couldn't break them.

Just then, a heavy cannon that was being stored in the hold broke loose and rolled across the floor, smashing through the hull of the ship. The angry ocean rushed in, pulling everything in its grasp back out through the hole. Bram clung to Mosey and felt her pull with all her strength . . .

And the chain snapped!

Boy and elephant were sucked into a swirling cold void, tumbling into darkness. There was no up or down, nothing to hold on to. Then—air! Bram gasped it in gratefully.

He looked around. He was floating on the surface of the ocean amidst pieces of wreckage. Alone. "Modoc!" he called. "MO!" Had she drowned?

Then he heard a voice. "Hello . . . over here!" Bram swam toward the sound. As he got closer, he saw a group of survivors from the ship clinging together, trying to stay afloat.

One of them, to his relief, was Jimmy. Bram gasped out the terrible story of Mosey's loss. He didn't know how long they'd be able to survive in the open water, but without Mo, he wasn't sure he cared.

And then he heard a familiar sound.

The trumpet of an elephant!

Then it came again. And then louder, closer. Everyone could hear it. Bram peered into the early-morning gloom and saw a huge, dark shadow in the distance.

"Mosey!" he screamed as the shadow drew closer. Swept by the current, she almost passed right by them, but the men formed a line in the water and Bram, at the end of it, stretched his hand out as far as he could.

"Mosey, trunk!" he called, and the elephant extended her trunk until Bram brushed the tip of it, and then grabbed on.

Everyone circled around her, holding on. Modoc was like a floating island.

For two days, they floated. Elephants are great swimmers, and they can float for as long as they can keep their trunks above water. The men made their shirts into ropes and laid them over Mosey's back, then tied themselves to the ropes. They were thirsty and hungry and afraid, but determined to survive.

Finally, a tugboat appeared in the fog. They were saved! One by one, the tugboat's crew helped the survivors on board. Jimmy, the next to last, held his hand out to Bram. "Come on, lad, let's go!"

"But what about Mo, Jimmy?"

"We'll have to come back for her, son."

But Bram refused to leave his friend. He could see the tugboat was too small for Modoc to board. Jimmy turned to the ship's captain. "This elephant saved all our lives. We have to help her!"

The captain shrugged. "We must go. A new storm is brewing."

"You go on, Jimmy," Bram called.

"No, Bram, no!" Jimmy cried.

"Safe journey!" Bram shouted.

As the tugboat started to move away, Bram and Modoc drifted into the fog and were gone.

Bram lost count of the days as he and Modoc floated alone. He was sure that the captain of the tugboat would radio to another ship—but would Mosey's strength last long enough for them to see it in time? Her trunk began to sag beneath the water.

Bram tried to hold it up so she could breathe, but it was too heavy.

Holding tight to his friend, Bram whispered to her, "Mosey, girl, it's time to go. Don't be afraid." With her trunk firmly wrapped around his arm, they began to sink beneath the waves.

The next thing Bram knew, his arm was torn from Mosey's grasp. He felt himself being lifted up, up out of the water. There were men, bright lights, the sound of a horn.

Modoc's body was being raised out of the water by a huge chain. It was the last thing Bram saw before he slipped into unconsciousness.

When Bram opened his eyes again, he found himself in a bed, with a brown-skinned man in a turban looking over him. "Welcome, young sir," the man said. "My name is Sabu."

"Where am I?" Bram wanted to know.

"You are in the palace of His Majesty Karim Shankor, the Maharajah of Vanusori," Sabu told him. "His Majesty heard of your travels and asked that you be brought here."

"Where is Mosey? Where is my elephant?"

"You will see your elephant tomorrow, but for now you must rest."

The next morning, Bram was taken to an elephantarium, where, lying on her side on a thick bed of straw, was Mosey.

Bram ran to her. "Mosey, Mosey, it's me!"

The huge elephant stretched out her trunk toward the sound of his voice.

Once she was reunited with Bram, the huge elephant's recovery was swift, and she was soon on her feet and following Bram and Sabu around the elephantarium gardens.

The maharajah summoned Bram to his palace for lunch that afternoon. "My boy, I am intrigued by the relationship you have with your Modoc—and through such perils. But isn't it true that Modoc belongs to an American circus?"

"I guess it is true," Bram admitted. "All I know is that we have to be together."

The maharajah was impressed with Bram's truthfulness and loyalty. "Until this matter is sorted out, you will be my guest for as long as you like."

Bram and Mosey learned that the other elephants were being specially trained to work in the teak forests, handling the heavy trees. Modoc began to work with them and was soon stronger than ever.

Then one day the maharajah summoned Bram.

"My boy, I have just received a distressing letter from a Mr. North who claims to be the owner of the elephant you call Modoc. He says that he is coming to retrieve his stolen property. I'm afraid it is my duty to place you and Modoc under house arrest until this man arrives."

His eyes began to twinkle. "However, I must also tell you that sometimes in the evenings my guards are prone to sleeping on duty."

With this the maharajah took a gold ring from his finger and placed it on Bram's hand. "You are my son in spirit. With the protection of this ring, all will welcome you and protect you wherever you go."

Bram hugged the maharajah and thanked him for all he had done for him and for Mosey. That very night, he and his elephant set off.

For over a month, Bram and Modoc wandered through India, heading south toward the forests where the great teak trees grew. Finally one morning they reached the top of a ridge and Bram looked down to see dozens of elephants hauling, stacking, and pulling teak logs out of the river.

When Bram asked for work, the overseer said he already had all the elephants he needed. "That's a fine big beast you have there, though," he admitted. "Maybe I could train her to do some of the heavy work."

Bram showed him the ring that the maharajah had given him, and explained that both he and Modoc already knew how to work with teak. He begged for a chance to show what he and Mosey could do, and the overseer finally agreed.

"Gather round!" he called to his workers. "Let's watch them perform—it should be good entertainment if nothing else!" Modoc's superior size, along with the grace she had acquired from her years of circus performing, made her naturally adept at balancing, lifting, and pulling the heavy teak logs. And of course, she obeyed all of Bram's commands to the letter. The *mahouts* all cheered when she completed the test, and the overseer admitted he had been wrong.

"You're both hired!"

Life in the teak camp was all Bram had hoped it would be. The work was hard, but the elephants were treated well, and the mahouts were a friendly bunch. But one day Bram was awakened by the sound of gunshots.

He came out of his bungalow to find the camp surrounded by ragged-looking men in military uniform. "We have just taken over your village in the name of the people of Pakistan," their leader said. "Saddle fifteen of your best elephants and load them up with food and ammunition. Tomorrow morning you will join our caravan and help us to attack the Indian army."

They had no choice but to accompany the armed men.

The guerrillas forced the elephants to carry their heavy loads for days and nights with little food and less rest along a steep trail through the mountains. They would surely have worked them all to death. But before they reached the next village, Indian fighter planes flew overhead, spraying the caravan with bullets! Modoc was shot twice in the skull. She still managed to make it to the Indian army camp, though, along with most of the other elephants and their mahouts.

Luckily, Modoc's wounds were not too serious, and she and Bram were able to rest in the army hospital for a while. Bram wasn't sure what they'd do now, where they would go. But before he had time to think it over, he was in for another surprise.

"You have a visitor," the army doctor announced one day, and in walked a glaring Mr. North.

"Do you know what it's cost me in time and money to find you?" the circus owner demanded. "You're going to prison, boy, for kidnapping my elephant. As soon as her wounds are healed, she's coming with me on the next ship to New York!"

While Bram was in jail awaiting his trial, Mr. North tried to load Modoc onto the ship. The big elephant seemed very nervous, looking everywhere for her friend. When men came to lead her up the dock, she froze on the spot. Pushing and shoving couldn't move her an inch. When they tried to beat her with a club, she simply curled her massive trunk around the weapon and threw it away. Finally Mr. North was forced to send for Bram to be released from jail.

"You can come on the boat with us and keep this beast in order," he told him, "but if there is one bit of trouble, I will personally throw you both overboard! Understood?"

"Yes, sir," Bram told him with a huge smile. "Come on, Mosey, let's go!" And to the exasperation of Mr. North, the boy rode the huge elephant—now as docile as a kitten— right past him up the gangplank and onto the ship.

And so it was that a few weeks later, Modoc and Bram stood proudly together on the upper deck of the ship as it steamed past the Statue of Liberty and into the New York harbor.

Jay North presents
Modo

Over the next six months, Bram taught Modoc some of the most spectacular tricks an elephant was ever to do. Everyone wanted to see them, and before long, they were the stars of the Ringling Brothers Circus.

Their act was in the center ring—the place of honor. It was truly a proud moment for the pair who had come so far together.

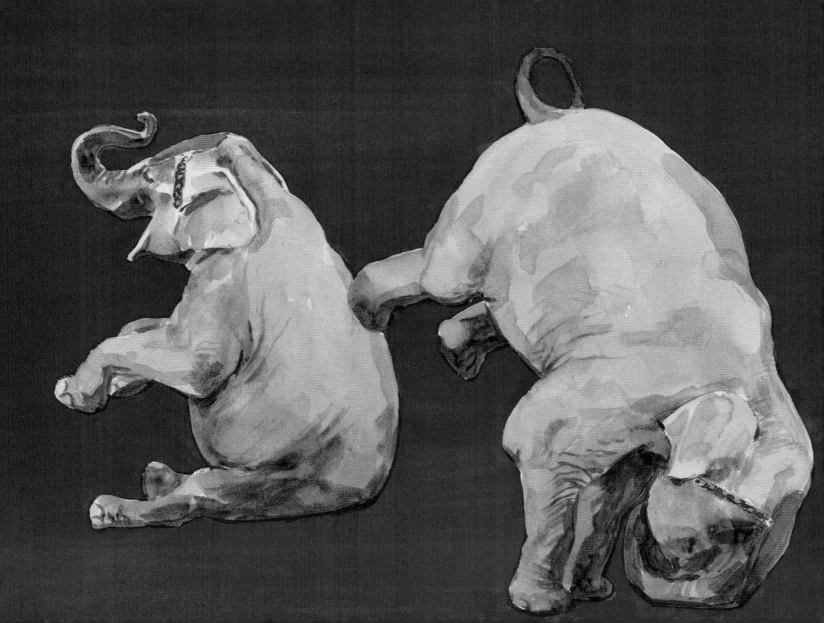

THE WORLD'S GREATEST ELEPHANT

Center Ring

Spectacular Tricks!!!

For many years, they traveled the States together. Audiences loved them wherever they went. And then, one fine May day, disaster struck again. Fire in the big top! Within minutes, the tent was ablaze. Hundreds of people, screaming in terror, blocked the exits and trampled one another in their desperate attempts to escape.

Bram gathered up as many children as he could find, and Modoc lifted them in her trunk and deposited them on her back, then carried them all out to safety. Bram and Mosey went back into the burning tent again and again, rescuing as many people as they could.

On their last trip, they raced for the open air and made it out just as the tent exploded in a fiery blaze.

Modoc was severely burned. Circus workers threw buckets of water on her smoking skin, but the fire had done its damage. It was many months before she could walk again, and huge white scars covered most of her body.

Mr. North called Bram into his office. "We can't have that ugly, scarred old beast in our show anymore," he said. "Put her out back until I decide what to do with her."

Bram went to the bank and drew out all his savings. "I would like to buy Modoc from you," he told Mr. North, putting the money on the table.

But Mr. North just looked at him, stone-faced. "No. Never."

Later that day, without telling Bram, he secretly sold Modoc to a man who came and took her away in the middle of the night.

Bram begged Mr. North to tell him who had bought her, but the circus owner would not.

Instead Mr. North fired him from the circus and barred him from the premises. Brokenhearted, Bram set out alone to search for his friend.

He began hitching rides around the country and working on farms when he needed money. Everywhere he went, he put up posters and took out ads in the newspaper asking for information about the whereabouts of a giant, scarred elephant, but to no avail.

Ten years passed.

"Elephant for sale. Cheap." That was all the ad said. A rancher who trained animals and rented them out to the motion picture industry saw it in the paper, and drove his truck up into the Ozark Mountains to check it out.

"She's a mean old thing," the man who had placed the ad told him. "You can have her for a thousand bucks if you want her, but be careful. She's a killer."

The rancher went around to the back of the house and was horrified by what he saw. A giant old elephant, skinny and covered with scars, was chained to an oak tree. Kids were throwing rocks at her.

The man ran them off and approached the poor old beast. He offered her food, but she seemed hungrier for affection, and allowed the gentle stranger to lead her away without protest. The rancher had to take the chain as well; the links of it were embedded in her leg, she'd been wearing it for so long.

No one expected the elephant would work, but the rancher and his staff thought they were doing a kindness by allowing her to live out her last days in comfort. Then one day, the rancher left a radio on near her stall. The sound of a circus calliope came on.

The old elephant began to dance! She swayed and trumpeted, waving her trunk in time to the music. "She must have been a circus performer!" the rancher marveled. He began to work with her, and discovered that she still knew many tricks.

It was about a year later that a weather-beaten old man came by the ranch, asking for work. "I used to train circus animals," he explained to the rancher. "Maybe I could help out around here."

"Ever work with elephants?" the rancher asked, leading the way to the fields where the elephants were trained.

The man's eyes brightened as he walked among them. "I once worked with the greatest elephant that ever lived. Maybe you've even heard of her—her name was Modoc."

Just then came a loud, bellowing trumpet. An elephant by the fence had heard her name.

"Modoc? MODOC?" Bram cried. "It can't be!"

But it was! She broke past the fences, nearly ran him over, then swung him up in her trunk, rumbling with joy. After all those years, Modoc and Bram were together again.